SIGNAL FLAGS

MYSTIC
SEAPORT

THE MUSEUM

OF AMERICA

AND THE SEA

© Mystic Seaport   2015 ISBN: 978-0-939511-42-6

All rights reserved. No part of this publication may be reproduced or transmitted in any form or by any means, electronic or mechanical, including photocopy, recording, or any other information storage and retrieval system, without prior permission in writing from the publisher.

The Language of the
Sea Winds

How can ships communicate on the open sea? For more than 100 years radio and then satellite communications have been used to speak between ships, and signal lights have long been used for simple messages, but even today ships speak the language of flags.

For the first few thousand years of seafaring, ships of war had the greatest need to communicate. To distinguish friend from foe at sea, flags represented a ship's allegiance to a king or city—which eventually evolved into national ensigns. Naval commanders might send orders to their fleets using lanterns or flags at different locations in the rigging.

An act of Congress in July 1866 required that US merchant ships each be given an official number and a set of signal letters, originally four flags beginning with one of the consonants H through W, a system that gave more that 53,000 combinations. For example, the whaleship *Charles W. Morgan* was assigned the signal letters JBPN, which she still flies almost 150 years later. With this system, captains could refer to annual publications to identify vessels they passed and exchange messages that both captains could quickly decipher.

Large yachts also received official numbers and signal letters, and yacht clubs used the same signal flags to communicate while racing and cruising. In the New York Yacht Club, the racing signal R meant "man overboard"; when cruising, BR meant "wish you a pleasant voyage"; and as a general signal ER meant "there is fog outside." With some revisions, many of these yachting signals are still used.

US Navy and other government vessels were also assigned signal letters, so the USS *Constitution* is NAPJ. As the *Constitution*'s hoist indicates, code flags for vowels were added to the alphabet in 1901, as well as three repeater or substitute pennants to allow double letter combinations. This code was revised through international agreement in 1889, and in

1927 its messages were expanded to include English, French, Italian, German, Japanese, Norwegian, and Spanish phrases.

From 1914 to 1990, two world wars and a cold war again emphasized naval power, naval signaling became even more complicated, and naval and commercial codes diverged. Today, commercial signaling is controlled by the International Maritime Organization (IMO), which simplified its vocabulary to emphasize safety and navigation in 1969, in light of the development of electronic communication. Much of the world's naval signaling is under the authority of the North Atlantic Treaty Organization (NATO), codified in its *Allied Maritime Signal and Maneuvering Book.*

But no matter whether it's a navy or a merchant ship, if you see the vertical yellow and blue bars of the K (kilo) flag flying under the code pennant, you'll know the message: "I wish to communicate."

Andrew W. German
Mystic, Connecticut
August 2014

Alpha

I have a diver down; keep well clear at low speed.

Bravo

I am taking in, discharging, or carrying dangerous cargo.

Charlie

"Yes" or "affirmative."

Delta

I am maneuvering with difficulty; keep clear.

Echo

I am directing my course to starboard.

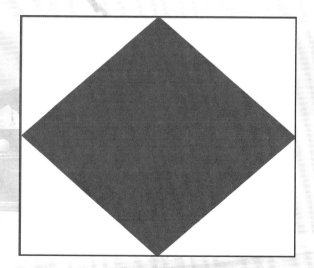

Foxtrot

I am disabled; communicate with me. On aircraft carriers: Flight operations underway.

Golf

I require a pilot.

Hotel

I have a pilot on board.

India

Coming alongside.

Juliett

I am on fire and have dangerous cargo; keep clear.

Kilo

I wish to communicate with you.

You should stop your vessel immediately.

Mike

My vessel is stopped; making no way.

November

No or negative.

Oscar

Man overboard.

Papa

All personnel return to ship; proceeding to sea.

Quebec

Boat recall; all boats return to ship.

Romeo

Preparing to replenish (at sea). Ready duty ship.

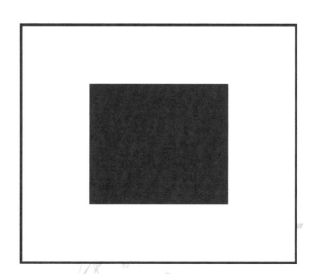

Sierra

Conducting flag hoist drill.

Tango

Do not pass ahead of me.

Uniform

You are running into danger.

Victor

I require assistance.

Whiskey

I require medical assistance.

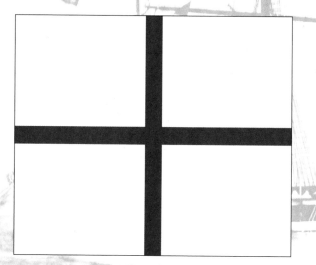

Xray

Stop carrying out your intentions and watch for my signals.

Yankee

Ship has visual communications duty.

Zulu

I require a tug.

1st Substitute

Absence of flag officer or unit commander.

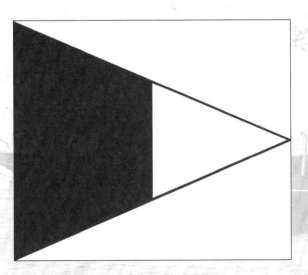

2nd Substitute

Absence of chief of staff.

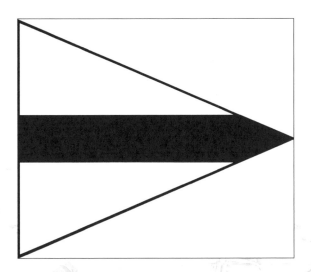

3rd Substitute

Absence of commanding officer.

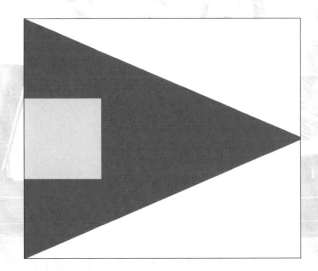

4th Substitute

Absence of civil or military official whose flag is flying on this ship.

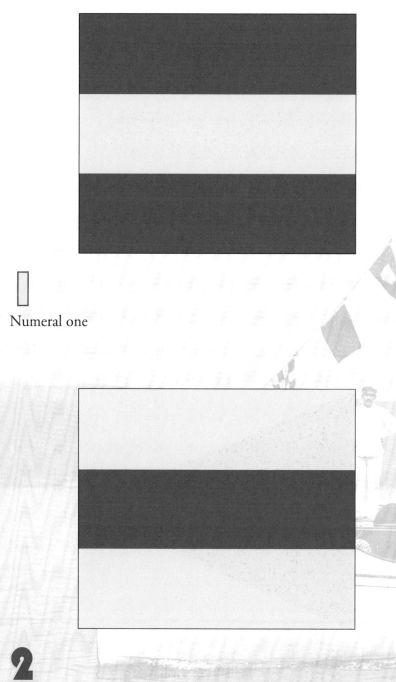

Numeral one

Numeral two

3

Numeral three

4

Numeral four

5

Numeral five

6

Numeral six

7

Numeral seven

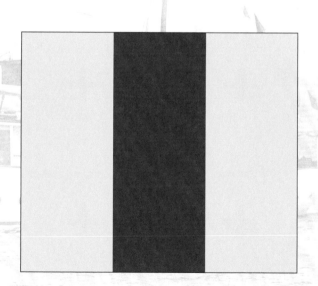

8

Numeral eight

9

Numeral nine

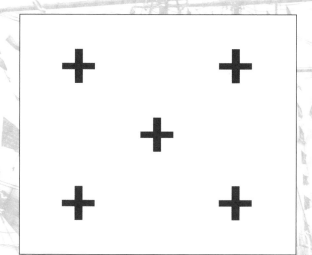

0

Numeral zero